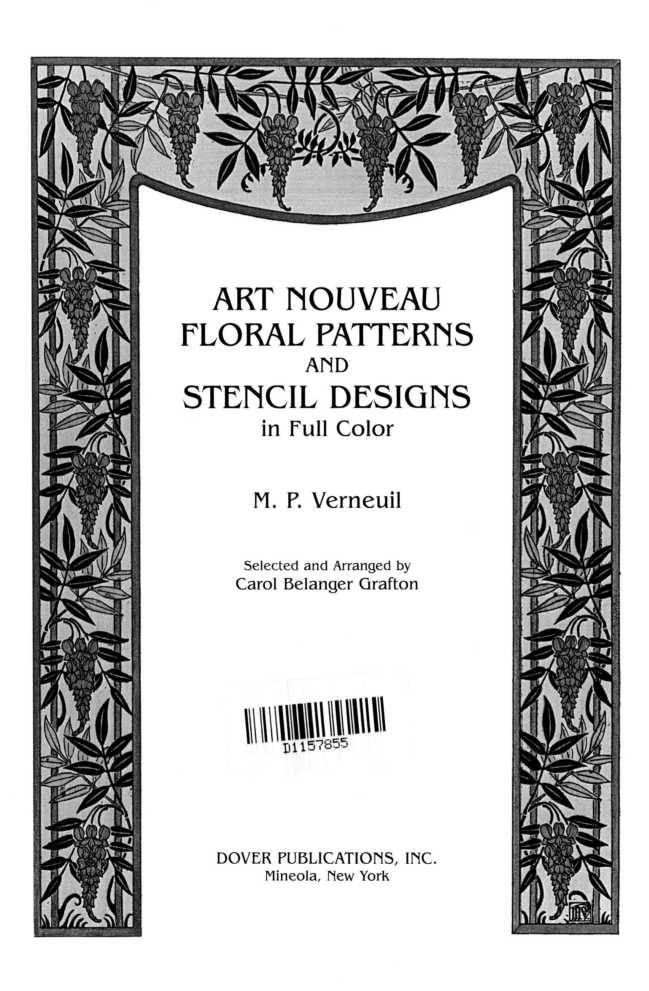

ART NOUVEAU FLORAL PATTERNS
AND
STENCIL DESIGNS
in Full Color

M. P. Verneuil

Selected and Arranged by
Carol Belanger Grafton

D1157855

DOVER PUBLICATIONS, INC.
Mineola, New York

Publisher's Note

At the turn of the century, M. P. Verneuil, an artist and an influential teacher of Art Nouveau decoration, made outstanding contributions to the use of design motifs and elements based on plant life. In *Art Nouveau Floral Patterns and Stencil Designs in Full Color,* for the first time are brought together a generous selection of his botanical designs for paper, textiles, ceramics, and stained glass, published in his magnificent *Étude de la Plante,* along with the complete set of floral stencil patterns by Verneuil published in Paris in the 1890s. Nearly 160 color plates present simple but highly evocative designs based on cultivated and wild flowers (focusing on leaves, stems, nuts, and seed pods, as well as blossoms) plus reeds and rushes, mushrooms, and even seaweed. In addition to large-scale and all-over patterns, borders, roundels, corners, and vignettes are included. Also featured are several of Verneuil's glorious paintings of the natural plants. The more than three dozen floral stencil designs (most of them created using only one or two stencils) are ideal for the decoration of wallpaper, fabric, stationery, wood, and other surfaces. Among them are several designs that include birds and insects, and one fluid pattern featuring fish. In their totality, the designs included—all based on elegant organic forms—combine the flowing, curvilinear style that became the hallmark of Art Nouveau with an imaginative use of geometric forms and abstract elements.

TITLE PAGE: 1. Wisteria. THIS PAGE: 2. Wood anemone.

2

Copyright

Copyright © 1998 by Dover Publications, Inc.
All rights reserved.

Bibliographical Note

This Dover edition, first published in 1998, includes a selection of illustrations from the work *Étude de la Plante: son application aux industries d'art,* published by the Librairie Centrale des Beaux-Arts, Paris, n.d. (ca. 1900) and all of the illustrations from the portfolio *L'ornementation par le Pochoir,* published by Schmid and Laurens, Paris, n.d. The Publisher's Note and captions in English are new features of the present edition.

DOVER *Pictorial Archive* SERIES

This book belongs to the Dover Pictorial Archive Series. You may use the designs and illustrations for graphics and crafts applications, free and without special permission, provided that you include no more than ten in the same publication or project. (For permission for additional use, please write to Permissions Department, Dover Publications, Inc., 31 East 2nd Street, Mineola, New York 11501.)

However, republication or reproduction of any illustration by any other graphic service, whether it be in a book or in any other design resource, is strictly prohibited.

International Standard Book Number
ISBN-13: 978-0-486-40126-3
ISBN-10: 0-486-40126-X

Manufactured in the United States by Courier Corporation
40126X05
www.doverpublications.com

3

4

3. Foxglove. **4.** Teasel.

5 & 6. Mistletoe. **7.** Water lily. **8.** Periwinkle. **9.** Species of iris. **10.** Columbine. **11.** Water lily.

8

10

9

11

5

12

13

12. Seaweed. **13.** Fig. **14.** Horn poppy. **15.** Virginia creeper.

14

15

16. Bittersweet (woody nightshade).
17. Bryony.

18. Daffodil. 19. Arrowhead. 20. Iris.

21. Cyclamen. **22.** Iris. **23.** Poppy. **24.** Lady's slipper. **25.** Bulrush.

23

24

25

11

26

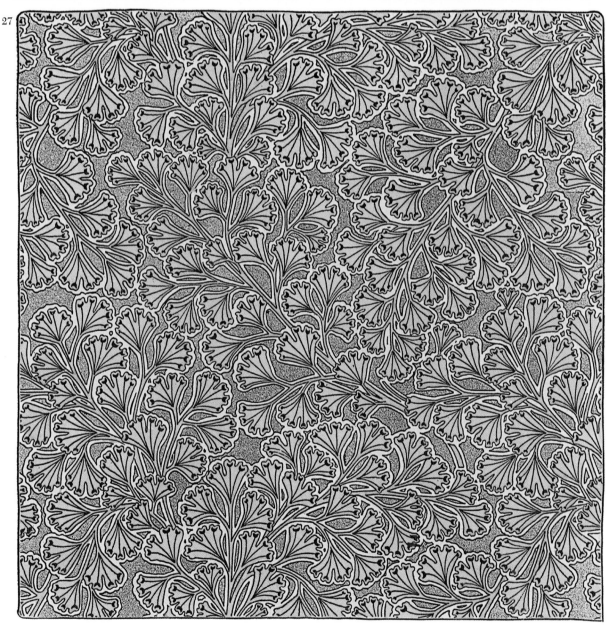

27

26. Fritillary. 27. Maidenhair fern. 28. Wild iris. 29. Columbine. 30. (Decorative corners.)

13

31. Martagon lily. **32.** Species of lily. **33.** Mushrooms. **34.** Fritillary.

33

34

15

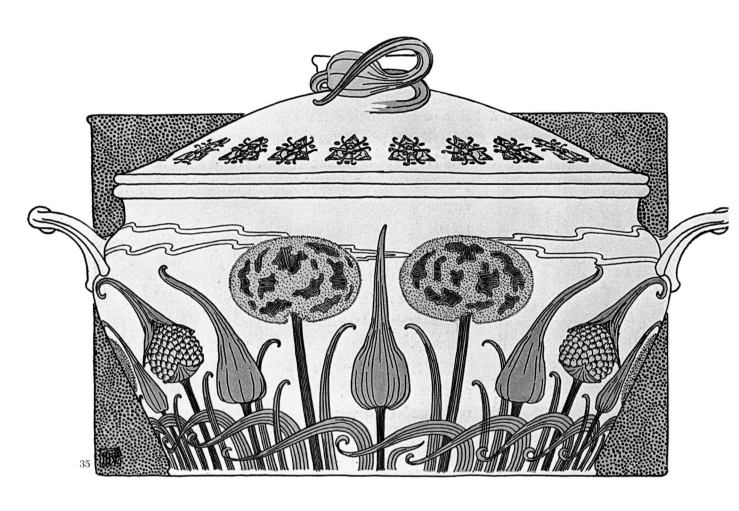

35. Leek. 36. Quaking grass. 37. Bellflower. 38. Plane tree. 39. Dandelion. 40. Horn poppy.
41. Fuchsia. 42. Lily of the valley. 43. Lady's slipper. 44. Cyclamen.

39

40

41

43

42

44

17

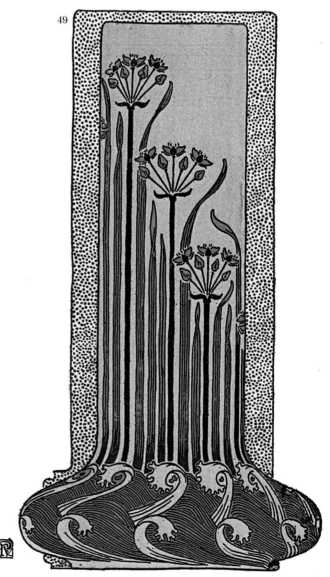

45. Bindweed. **46.** Fritillary. **47.** Freesia. **48.** Bellflower. **49.** Butomus (flowering rush).

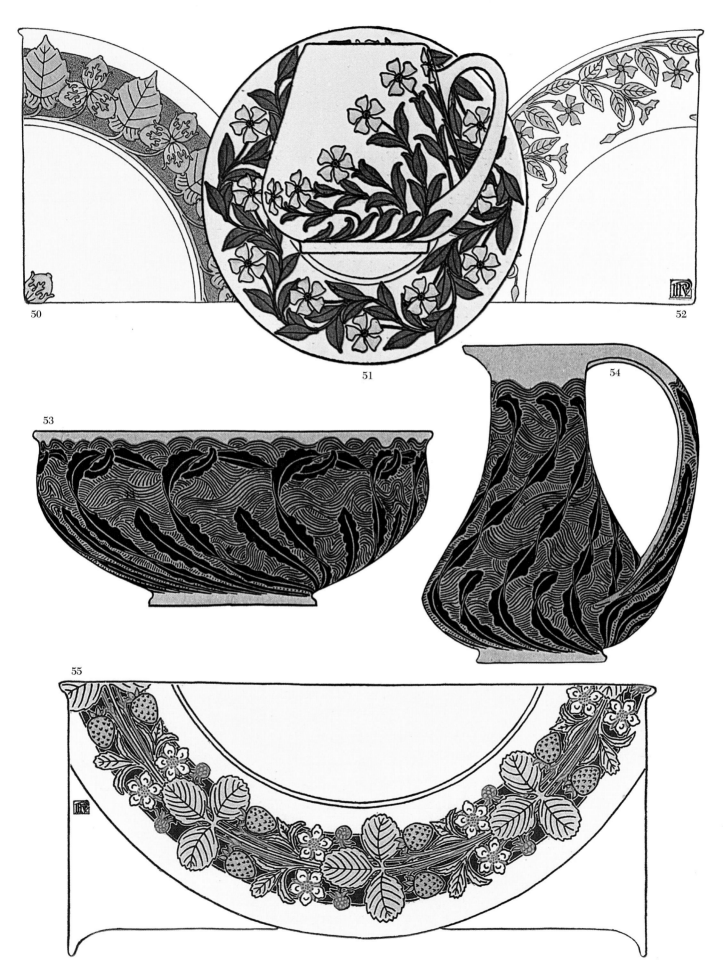

50. Hazel. **51 & 52.** Periwinkle. **53 & 54.** Green seaweed. **55.** Strawberry.

19

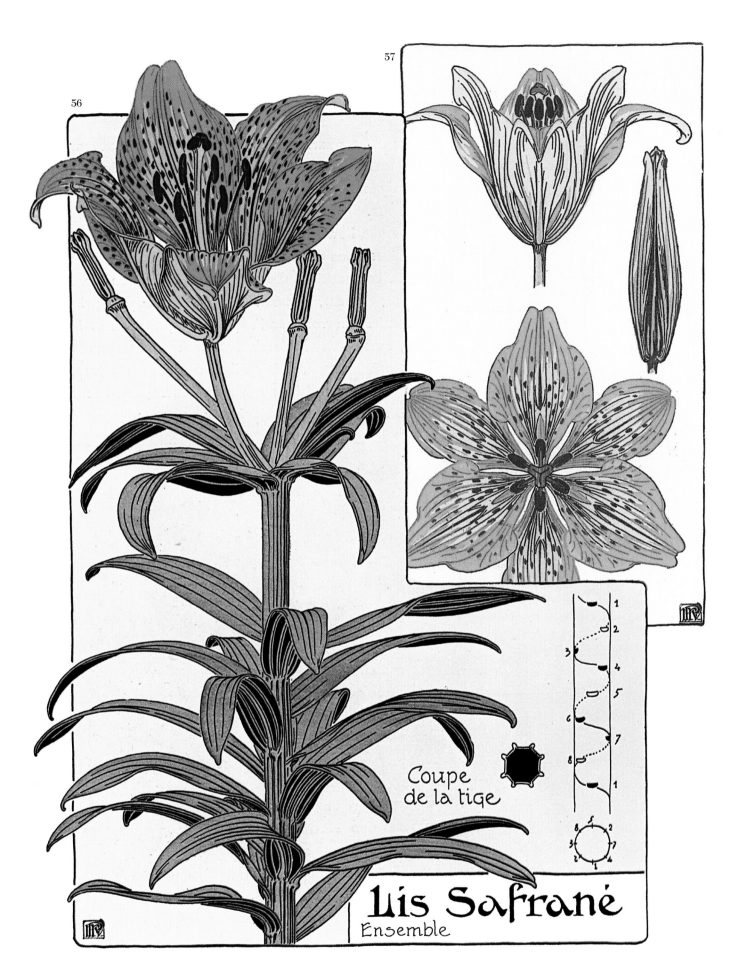

56

57

Coupe
de la tige

Lis Safrané
Ensemble

56 & 57. Species of lily.

Glycine

Arbrisseau grimpant atteignant
10ᵐ de hauteur. Feuilles vert jaune
Fleurs violet très pâle. Fleurit en
avril-mai.   Fig. 76.

59

Soleil
Detail de la fleur
et de la feuille.

60 Bolet blafard. Dessus brun chair éclat;
dessous rouge sang. Tige
blanc jaune, tachée
de points rouges.

15.ᵈ de
hauteur.

Champignons
Espèces diverses.

Fig. 311

22

Nénuphar blanc

Plante aquatique, aux feuilles flottantes, vertes; fleurs blanches. Fleurit de juin en septembre.

59. Sunflower. **60.** Mushroom of the genus *Boletus*. **61.** White water lily.

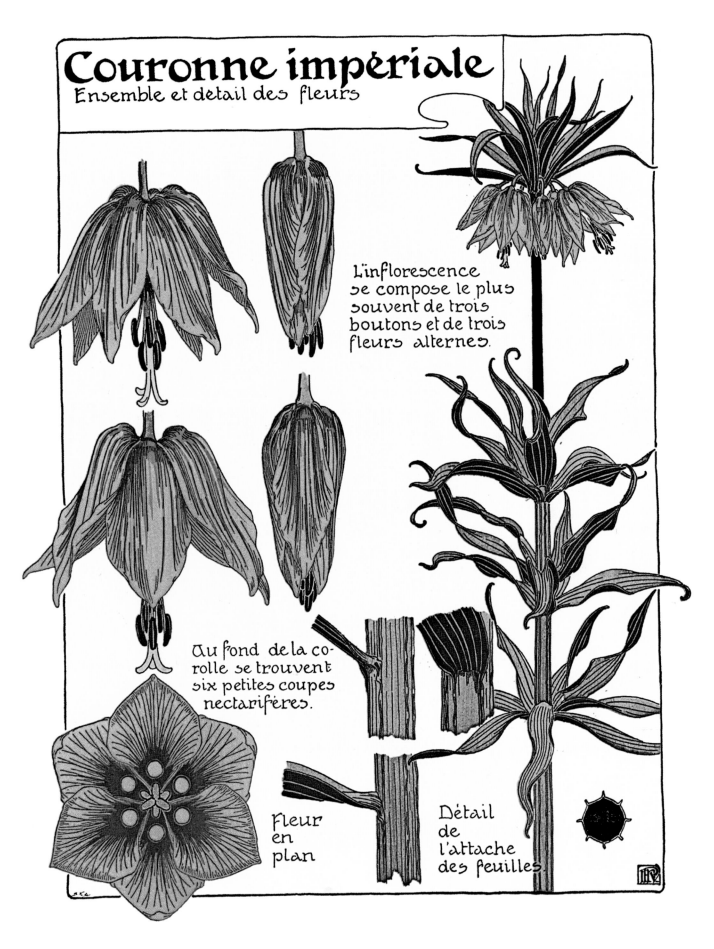

Couronne impériale

Ensemble et détail des fleurs

L'inflorescence se compose le plus souvent de trois boutons et de trois fleurs alternes.

Au fond de la corolle se trouvent six petites coupes nectarifères.

Fleur en plan

Détail de l'attache des feuilles

62. Crown imperial.

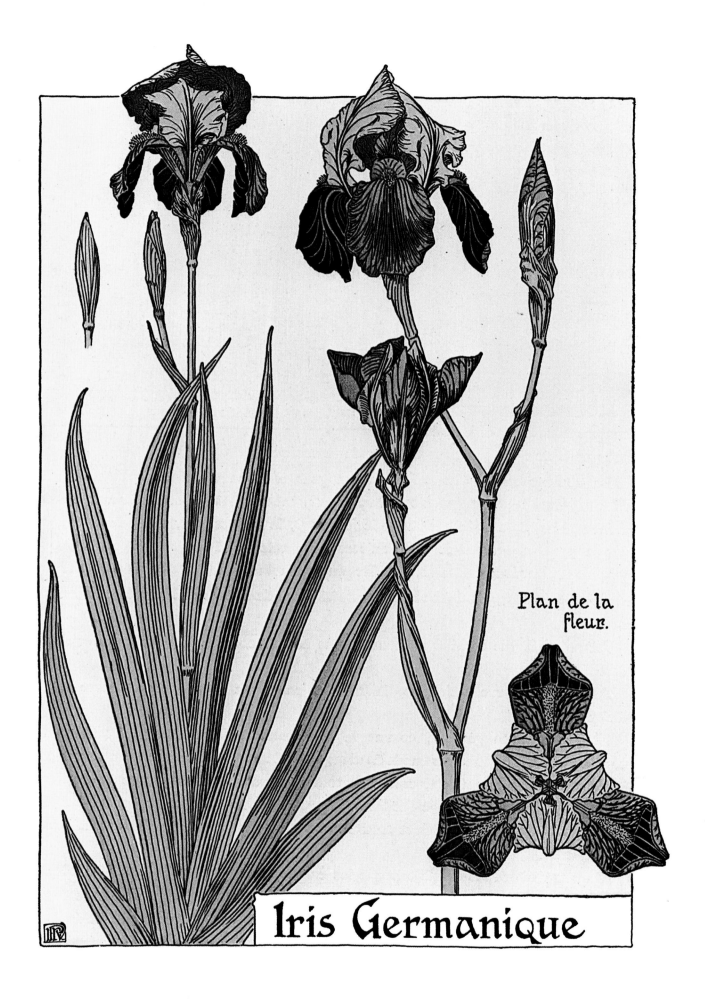

Plan de la
fleur.

Iris Germanique

63. Species of iris.

64

Grenadier

Arbrisseau du midi, haut de 3 à 4 m.
Feuilles vert froid, tiges rouges; fleurs
rouge vif; fruit vert, puis rouge violacé.

65

Pavot
Details.

Détail
des
dentelu-
res

66

67

64. "Grenadier," flowering shrub of the south of France. **65.** Poppy. **66.** (Decorative heading.)
67. Cyclamen.

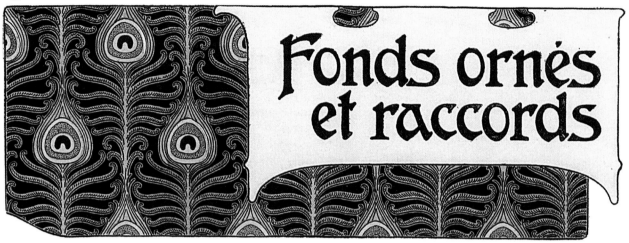

68

Fonds ornés et raccords

69

Vitrail

70

Papiers peints et étoffes imprimées

68–70. (Various decorative headings.)

71 Interprétation

72 Bordures

73 Étude de la plante

71–73. (Various decorative headings.)

74. Wood anemone. **75–77.** *Porillon* (French name). **78.** Hazel. **79.** Sunflower. **80.** Yellow water lily.

78

79

80

81. Species of iris.

82. (Decorative band.) 83 & 84. Columbine. 85. Maple.

86

87

88

86. Oleander. **87.** Castor-oil plant. **88.** Oak.

89

90

89. Sunflower. **90.** Hollyhock.

91. Apple. **92.** Wild orchid. **93.** Fuchsia. **94.** Chestnut.

95

96

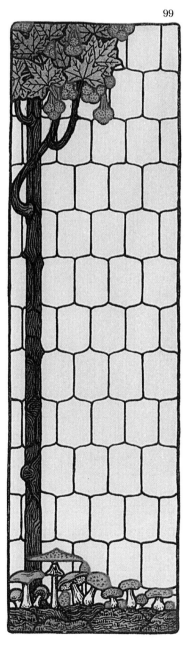

95. Milk thistle. **96.** Snowdrop. **97.** Tiger lily. **98 & 99.** Plane tree.

101

100. Wisteria. **101.** Loofah. **102.** Wood anemone. **103.** *Porillon* (French name). **104.** Gourd.

102

103

104

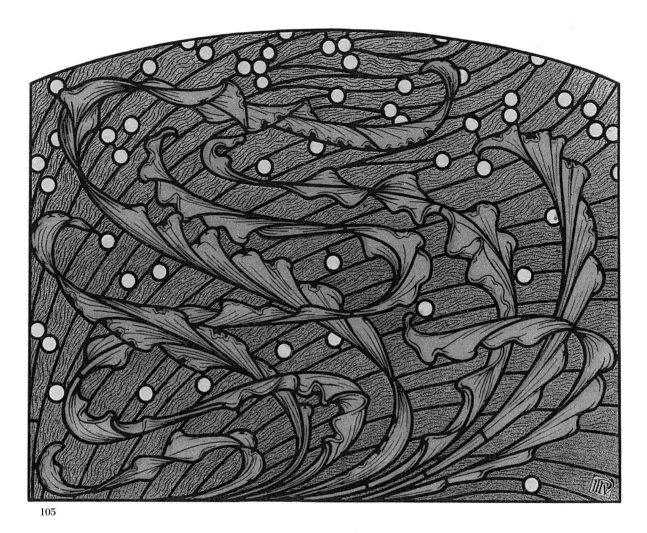

105

106

Céramique

105. Seaweed. **106.** (Decorative heading.) **107.** Cyclamen. **108.** Nasturtium.

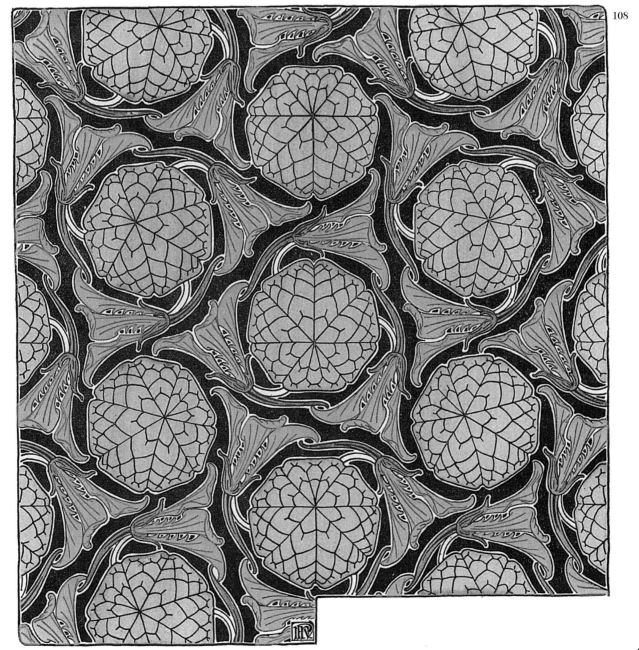

44   **109.** Bittersweet (woody nightshade). **110.** Coltsfoot. **111.** Pomegranate. **112.** Poppy.

111

112

113

114

115

116

113. Maple. 114. Lady's slipper. 115. Plane tree. 116. Water lily and arrowhead.

117. Tiger lily. 118. Coltsfoot.

47

119. Jasmine. **120.** Hollyhock.

121. Various flower-shaped ornaments.

122. Decorative borders, rosette, triangles, and corners.

50

123. Decorative border and powderings (spot ornaments).

124. Decorative border.

125. Periwinkle. 126. Wild hyacinth.

53

127. Poppy.

128. Chestnut.

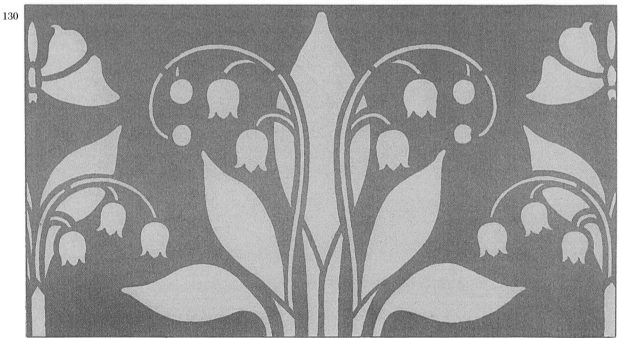

129 & 130. Lily of the valley and butterflies.

131. Decorative border and powderings.

132. Decorative borders.

133. Decorative corners.

134. Mistletoe. 135. Snowdrop.

136. Cyclamen.

138

137

62

137. Wood sorrel. 138. Clover.

139. Bindweed. 140. Wood sorrel.

141. Holly.

142. Oak.

143. Christmas rose

144. Anemone.

145. Ivy.

146. Lily and jonquil.

147. Bindweed and columbine.

148. Fish.

149. Iris and dragonflies.

150. Flowering rush.

151. Sunflower.

152. Iris. 153. Wild rose.

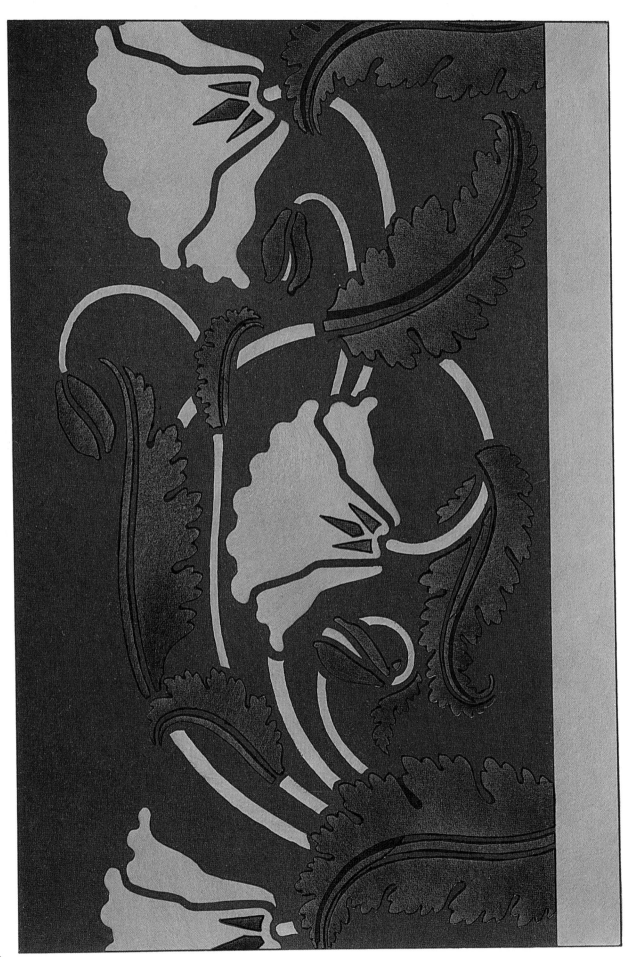

154. Poppy.